Flower Wings

Violet Fairy
Gets her Wings

By Elizabeth Dennis

Illustrated by Natalie Smillie

Ready-to-Read

SCHOLASTIC INC.

ISBN 978-1-338-32956-8

12 11 10 9 8 7 6 5 4 3 2 1   18 19 20 21 22 23

Printed in the U.S.A.   40

First Scholastic printing, September 2018

Welcome to the land of the Flower Wings!

Can you keep a secret?

Flower Wings are fairies with powers from flowers!

To most people,
they just look like
regular flowers.

Meet Violet Fairy!

She just got her wings.

If you can see them,

you are very special.

Rose Fairy invites

Violet to tea.

It starts to rain!

Rose gets wet.

Violet stays dry.

Water rolls off her!

"How did you do that?"

Rose asks.

"The wax coating on my leaves keeps me dry in the rain," Violet says.

Inside, Rose dries off
while Violet makes tea.

Drip, drip, drip!

Oh no! The roof is leaking.

Violet flies off to look for
something to fix the roof.

When she lands,

she hurts her leg!

"Ouch!" Violet says.

Moth wants to help!

He makes a bandage with

silk from his old cocoon.

"I feel better!"

Violet says.

"Silk is strong,"
Moth explains.
"It keeps silkworms safe
while they change
into moths."

Violet has an idea.

"Do you have extra silk?"

she asks Moth.

Moth and his friends have

lots of silk!

Violet weaves the silk into fabric.

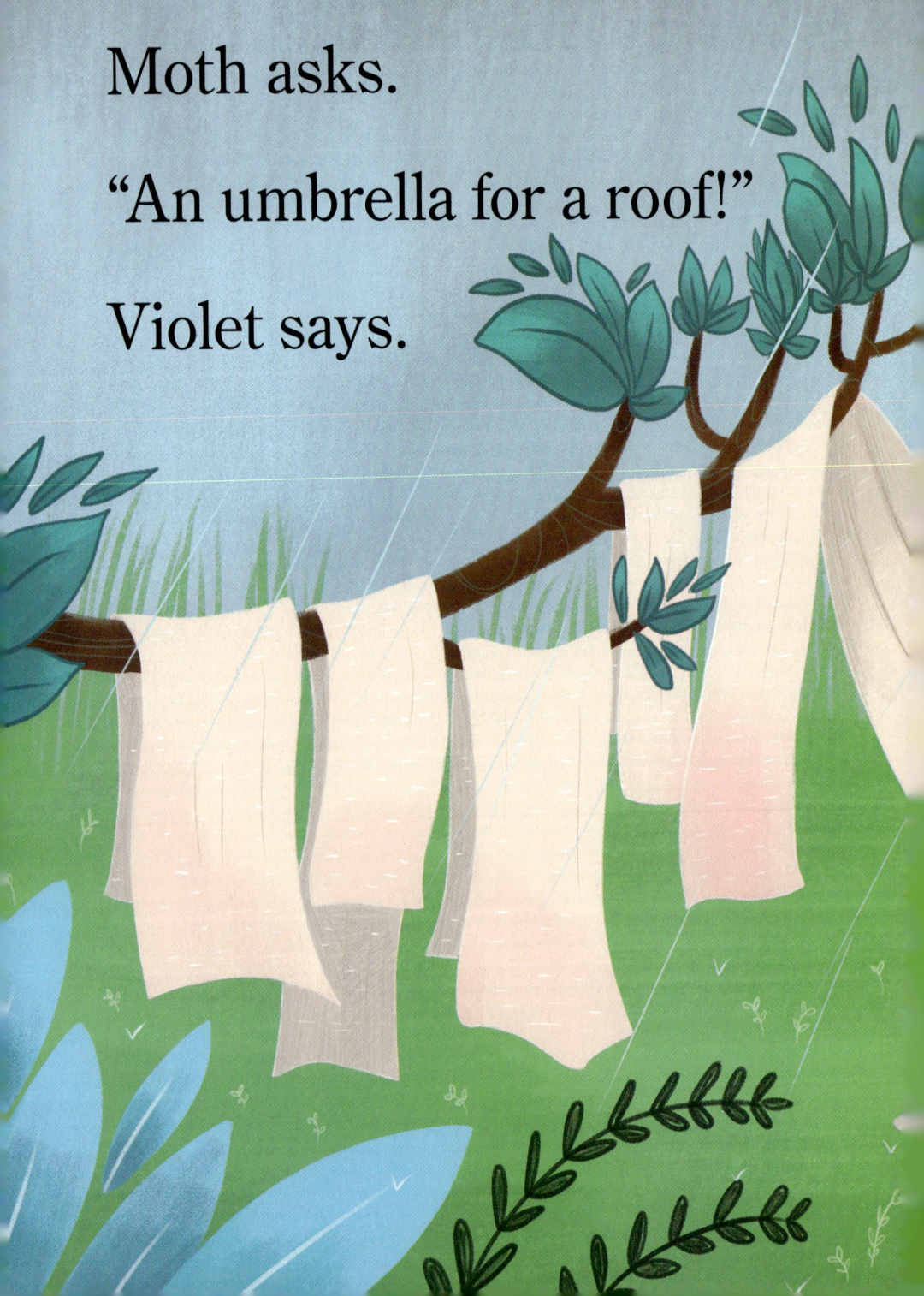

"What are you making?"

Moth asks.

"An umbrella for a roof!"

Violet says.

"Silk gets weak when it gets wet," Moth says. "The umbrella will leak!" Violet gasps. "I think I can protect the silk!"

Violet can use her power to protect the silk. She coats the fabric with wax so water rolls off it!

It works!

The umbrella will not leak!

"It is beautiful!"

Rose says.

"I used my power!"

Violet says proudly.

The rain stops, and the
sun comes out.

A rainbow appears
in the sky!

Thank you, Violet Fairy!

The Science behind the Story

Did you know:

Wild violets have strong roots and waxy leaves that make them tough, just like Violet Fairy!

How it works:

The waxy coating on wild violets helps them hold on to water for later.
It also protects them from some kinds of insects and pests. In gardens, it helps keep them safe from chemicals because some of the liquid rolls off the leaves.

The surprising secrets of silk:

Silk fabric is made out of strands of silk fiber. Those strands are made by a kind of caterpillar, called a silkworm, whose main source of food is leaves from mulberry trees.

In the larva stage, silkworms make cocoons using a single strand of silk fiber that comes out of a tube in their head! The cocoon protects them as they grow into silkworm moths.

Silk is harvested by unwinding the strand of fiber that makes up the cocoon. One strand can be as long as eight football fields!

The process for making fabric from silk was discovered in China between four and five thousand years ago!